W9-AAD-739

Be-good-to-yourself Therapy

Be-good-to-yourself Therapy

written by
Cherry Hartman

illustrated by
R.W. Alley

ONE
CARING
PLACE

Abbey Press

Text © 1987 by Cherry Hartman
Illustrations © 1987 St. Meinrad Archabbey
Published by One Caring Place
Abbey Press
St. Meinrad, Indiana 47577

All rights reserved.
No part of this book may be used or reproduced in any manner
without written permission of the publisher, except in the case of
brief quotations embodied in critical articles and reviews.

Library of Congress Catalog Number
87-72436

ISBN 0-87029-209-9

Printed in the United States of America

Foreword

In the course of growing up, many folks pick up attitudes that drag them down. Do you feel bad if you express anger? Are you ashamed of your feelings? Do you harass yourself if you make a mistake or fail? Do you experience guilt when you put your own needs before those of others? *Be-good-to-yourself Therapy* was written to help you overcome the distorted notions that keep you from living fully and honestly.

Although many people today may equate self-esteem with self-indulgence, genuine self-love begins with the recognition that each of us is God's handiwork. To love oneself is to express love for God, the Creator. What's more, you cannot be a gift to others unless you nurture your own spiritual, psychological, and physical well-being.

Be good to yourself—enjoy this book and let its rules free you for more peaceful, harmonious living.

1.

Trust yourself. You know what you want and need.

2.

Put yourself first. You can't
be anything for anybody else
unless you take care of yourself.

3.

Let your feelings be known.
They are important.

4.

Express your opinions.
It's good to hear yourself talk.

5.

Value your thinking.
You do it well.

6.

Take the time and space
you need—even if other people
are wanting something from you.

7.

When you need something,
don't talk yourself out of it.
Even if you can't have it,
it's OK to need.

8.

When you're scared,
let someone know. Isolating
yourself when you're scared
makes it worse.

9.

When you feel like running away,
let yourself feel the scare. Think
about what you fear will happen
and decide what you need to do.

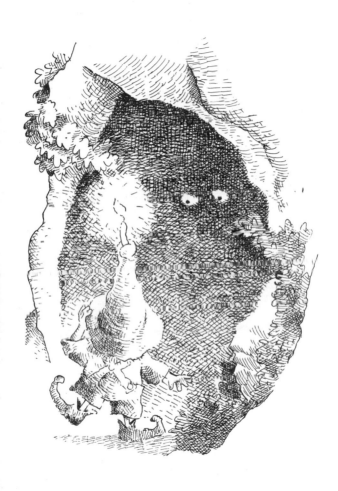

10.

When you're angry, let yourself
feel the anger. Decide what you
want to do: just feel it,
express it, or take some action.

11.

When you're sad, think about what would be comforting.

12.

When you're hurt, tell the person who hurt you. Keeping it inside makes it grow.

13.

When you see someone else's
hurt face, breathe. You are
not responsible for making
other people happy.

14.

When you have work to do and you don't want to do it, decide what really needs to be done and what can wait.

15.

When you want something from someone else, ask. You'll be OK if they say no. Asking is being true to yourself.

16.

When you need help, ask.
Trust people to say no if they
don't want to give.

17.

When people turn you down,
it usually has to do with them
and not with you. Ask someone
else for what you need.

18.

When you feel alone, know there
are people who want to be with you.
Fantasize what it would be like
to be with each of them. Decide
if you want to make that happen.

19.

When you feel anxious,
let yourself know that in your
head you've moved into the future
to something scary and your body
has gotten up the energy for it.
Come back to the present.

20.

When you want to say something loving to someone, go ahead. Expressing your feelings is not a commitment.

21.

When someone yells at you, physically support yourself by relaxing into your chair or putting your feet firmly on the floor. Remember to breathe. Think about the message they are trying to get across to you.

22.

When you're harassing yourself, stop. You do it when you need something. Figure out what you need and get it.

23.

When everything seems wrong,
you are overwhelmed and need some
comforting. Ask for it.
Afterwards, you can think about
what you need to do.

24.

When you want to talk to someone
new and are scared, breathe.
Don't start rehearsing, just
plunge in. If it doesn't go well,
you can stop.

25.

If you're doing something you
don't like to do (such as smoking
or overeating), stop. Think
about what you really want.
If you're stuck and can't think
clearly, talk out loud to someone.

26.

When you can't think straight,
stop thinking. Feel.

27.

When you're in need of love,
reach out. There are people
who love you.

28.

When you're confused, it's usually because you think you should do one thing and you want to do another. Dialogue with yourself out loud or on paper, or present both sides to a friend.

29.

When you feel harried, slow down. Deliberately slow your breathing, your speech, and your movements.

30.

When you have tears, cry.

31.

When you feel like crying and
it's not a safe place to cry,
acknowledge your pain and promise
yourself a good cry later.
Keep your promise.

32.

When somebody does you wrong,
be actively angry with them.

33.

When everything seems gray,
look for color.

34.

When you feel like a baby,
take care of the baby in you.

35.

When somebody gives you a gift,
say "thank you." That's all
you need to do. A gift is not
an obligation.

36.

When somebody loves you, just accept and be glad. Love is not an obligation. You don't have to do anything in return.

37.

If one of these rules seems wrong for you, talk about it with someone. Then, rewrite it so it fits for you.

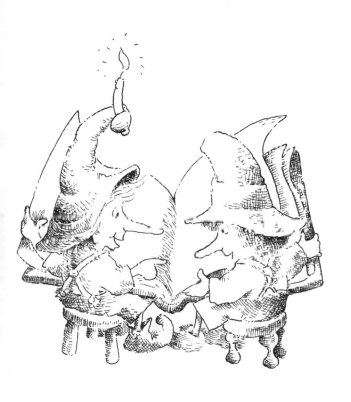

Cherry Hartman is a clinical social worker who has counseled individuals and couples, trained and supervised mental health professionals, and led workshops for over twenty years. She lives and works in Portland, Oregon. She is also the author of *More Be-good-to-yourself Therapy*.

Illustrator for the Abbey Press Elf-help Books, **R.W. Alley** also illustrates and writes children's books. He lives in Barrington, Rhode Island, with his wife, daughter, and son.

The Story of the Abbey Press Elves

The engaging figures that populate the Abbey Press "elf-help" line of publications and products first appeared in 1987 on the pages of a small self-help book called *Be-good-to-yourself Therapy*. Shaped by the publishing staff's vision and defined in R.W. Alley's inventive illustrations, they lived out author Cherry Hartman's gentle, self-nurturing advice with charm, poignancy, and humor.

Reader response was so enthusiastic that more Elf-help Books were soon under way, a still-growing series that has inspired a line of related gift products.

The especially endearing character featured in the early books—sporting a cap with a mood-changing candle in its peak—has since been joined by a spirited female elf with flowers in her hair.

These two exuberant, sensitive, resourceful, kindhearted, lovable sprites, along with their lively elfin community, reveal what's truly important as they offer messages of joy and wonder, playfulness and co-creation, wholeness and serenity, the miracle of life and the mystery of God's love.

With wisdom and whimsy, these little creatures with long noses demonstrate the elf-help way to a rich and fulfilling life.

Elf-help Books

...adding "a little character" and a lot of help to self-help reading!

Gratitude Therapy
#20105 $4.95   ISBN 0-87029-332-X

Garden Therapy
#20116 $4.95   ISBN 0-87029-325-7

Elf-help for Busy Moms
#20117 $4.95   ISBN 0-87029-324-9

Trust-in-God Therapy
#20119 $4.95   ISBN 0-87029-322-2

Elf-help for Overcoming Depression
#20134 $4.95   ISBN 0-87029-315-X

New Baby Therapy
#20140 $4.95   ISBN 0-87029-307-9

Grief Therapy for Men
#20141 $4.95   ISBN 0-87029-306-0

Living From Your Soul
#20146 $4.95   ISBN 0-87029-303-6

Teacher Therapy
#20145 $4.95   ISBN 0-87029-302-8

Be-good-to-your-family Therapy
#20154 $4.95   ISBN 0-87029-300-1

Stress Therapy
#20153 $4.95   ISBN 0-87029-301-X

Making-sense-out-of-suffering Therapy
#20156 $4.95   ISBN 0-87029-296-X

Get Well Therapy
#20157 $4.95   ISBN 0-87029-297-8

Anger Therapy
#20127 $4.95   ISBN 0-87029-292-7

Caregiver Therapy
#20164 $4.95   ISBN 0-87029-285-4

Self-esteem Therapy
#20165 $4.95   ISBN 0-87029-280-3

Take-charge-of-your-life Therapy
#20168 $4.95   ISBN 0-87029-271-4

Work Therapy
#20166 $4.95   ISBN 0-87029-276-5

Everyday-courage Therapy
#20167 $4.95   ISBN 0-87029-274-9

Peace Therapy
#20176 $4.95   ISBN 0-87029-273-0

Friendship Therapy
#20174 $4.95   ISBN 0-87029-270-6

Christmas Therapy (color edition)
#20175 $5.95   ISBN 0-87029-268-4

Grief Therapy
#20178 $4.95   ISBN 0-87029-267-6

Happy Birthday Therapy
#20181 $4.95   ISBN 0-87029-260-9

Forgiveness Therapy
#20184 $4.95   ISBN 0-87029-258-7

Keep-life-simple Therapy
#20185 $4.95   ISBN 0-87029-257-9

Be-good-to-your-body Therapy
#20188 $4.95   ISBN 0-87029-255-2

Celebrate-your-womanhood Therapy
#20189 $4.95   ISBN 0-87029-254-4

Acceptance Therapy (color edition)
#20182 $5.95   ISBN 0-87029-259-5

Acceptance Therapy
#20190 $4.95   ISBN 0-87029-245-5

Keeping-up-your-spirits Therapy
#20195 $4.95   ISBN 0-87029-242-0

Play Therapy
#20200 $4.95   ISBN 0-87029-233-1

Slow-down Therapy
#20203 $4.95   ISBN 0-87029-229-3

One-day-at-a-time Therapy
#20204 $4.95   ISBN 0-87029-228-5

Prayer Therapy
#20206 $4.95   ISBN 0-87029-225-0

Be-good-to-your-marriage Therapy
#20205 $4.95   ISBN 0-87029-224-2

Be-good-to-yourself Therapy (hardcover)
#20196 $10.95   ISBN 0-87029-243-9

Be-good-to-yourself Therapy
#20255 $4.95   ISBN 0-87029-209-9

Available at your favorite giftshop or bookstore—
or directly from One Caring Place, Abbey Press
Publications, St. Meinrad, IN 47577.
Or call 1-800-325-2511.